The Black Community's Quest for Equality "Resolving Poverty in the Black Community"

Embracing Diversity

by

Dr. Sandra Jenise Dailey

DORRANCE
PUBLISHING CO
EST. 1920
PITTSBURGH, PENNSYLVANIA 15238

Dorrance Publishing Co
585 Alpha Drive
Pittsburgh, PA 15238
Visit our website at *www.dorrancebookstore.com*

ISBN: 978-1-6495-7060-4
EISBN: 978-1-6495-7000-0

This book is dedicated

To my four children:
Dearie, Deidre, Tracy Jr. Sandra #2
and five grandchildren
Dearyuana, Dearyajah Deariah, Camron, and Summer.

Thanks to my mother Mary Dailey for believing in me.

To Spiritual and Professional leaders throughout the Universe,
especially my husband, Pastor Andrew Cannon.

Contents

Introduction

The passion for helping hurting people, that has always burned deep inside me, has begun to stir again. While walking through my old neighborhood, I was reminded why I have spent most of my adult life working to empower people in need. I was reminded that poverty in America is not just an issue of compassion. It is a social justice issue that needs to be corrected.

Most people are shocked when I tell my story of growing up in extreme poverty because I do not look like what I have been through. Poverty and minorities have negative images associated with them and it must change. The best way to change it is to be a part of programs and initiatives that support low-income people and to keep sharing personal stories with peers about those life-changing experiences. Intervention for poverty in the Black church and communities, entails, but is not limited to, providing the quality service that they deserve, while advocating for social change and justice for all.

Neighborhoods with poor-quality housing, few resources, and unsafe conditions impose stress, which can lead to depression. The stress imposed by adverse neighborhoods increases depression above and beyond the effects of the individual's own personal stressors, such as poverty and negative events within the family or workplace. Furthermore, adverse neighborhoods appear to intensify the harmful impact of personal stressors and interfere with the formation of bonds between people, again increasing risk for depression. Neighborhoods do not affect all people in the same way. People with different personality characteristics adjust in diverse ways to challenging neighborhoods (Hooks, 2000). Again, one would ask, did I research this conclusion, sure, but

I did not have to, because I grew up in this neighborhood as a very depressed child and adolescent.

No one can say that Christianity has failed, it has not. There are people from all races, cultures and institutions that continue to advocate for social and economic justice. Most of these entities identify as Christians.

My Story Part One

To appeal to the reader's sensibility, the personal story that follows is associated with this writer. Unless one has lived in extreme poverty, the story may seem to be fabricated. Until you are challenged with poverty, oppression, fear, and racism, the story may seem aloof.

This is the case of a Black female, who became pregnant at age fourteen. This narrative will present factors affecting the female's transition from adolescent to becoming a teenage mother as well as her social class, race, and ethnicity during her transition. This off-timed transition will present the biological, cognitive, and psychological issues that the young mother was challenged with. The developmental stages will also be presented.

Teenage pregnancy is defined as "a teenager girl, usually within the age of 13-19, becoming pregnant" (Akella and Jordan, 2015). A child having a baby as a teenager is more likely to face critical social issues like poverty, poor education, risky behaviors that lead to poor health issues, and child welfare. The United States has the highest level of teenage pregnancy amongst the industrialized nations. The level of teenage pregnancy is highest among the minority population (Akella and Jordan, 2015). Becoming pregnant at fourteen years old and having anemia was very unhealthy. This condition put the teenager and the unborn child at risk. Another risk factor currently was poor nutrition because of poverty.

One relevant theory of this transition is the conflict theory. As a fourteen-year-old child, I was still in the care of my parents. Usually children inherited the poverty of family. The parents were uneducated, poor, and had limited access to opportunity. The inheritance from parents were limited growth experiences, limited protection from predators, poor health care, and limited knowledge of physical development (Rogers, 2013).

Being the child of alcoholics, also attributed to increased domestic violence in the home. These contributing factors had a negative impact on views, values, beliefs, attitudes, and behaviors. Although the system was at best, described as one of entropy, I was able to transition to a system of negative entropy as a young adult.

Early puberty is associated with stressful family environment, early sexual intercourse, and racial background (De Genna, Larkby and Cornelius, 2011). Black females normally reach puberty around a year ahead of white females (De Genna et.al, 2011). Becoming a mother at age fourteen is very much off-time according to Erickson's theory. Erickson's theory identifies stage five as being the adolescence identity versus identity confusion (Rogers, 2013). During this time of growth, a teenager is discovering who they are. Teenagers are determining self-identity. Some teenagers have a tough time integrating their roles into their identity; this causes confusion.

Becoming pregnant during this time of transition magnifies the confusion. Being pregnant is an extraordinary event that is accompanied by abnormal stressors. As a Black female living with a poor family that did not have the means to support the existing dependents, trauma was added to the entire family, by my becoming pregnant.

During this time in my life, I was not mature enough to make decisions for myself. Most teenagers are not qualified to make decisions for another human being. According to Brien, Loya, and Pepper (2002) teenage childbearing is a symptom of low socioeconomic status. More African American girls are likely to engage in sexual activities than their white counterparts due to negative environmental factors.

The social learning theory is appropriate to use during this transition. As a fourteen-year-old, the writer interacted with the environment and learned from it. Unfortunately, mostly everything in my environment was negative, therefore; influencing me to make poor decisions as an adolescent.

This teenager learned through watching older sisters that it was cool to have a boyfriend; she did not understand the ramifications of being involved with the other sex. She learned from parents that it was okay to be irresponsible if what one was doing made her happy. This teenager was a young adult before she independently learned self-efficacy. She began to watch people of different races, ethnicities, and socioeconomic status to build a sense of competence.

This teenager was not aware of the detrimental effects that becoming a teen mother would have on her later developmental opportunities. Because of becoming a teen mother, she was forced to quit school and take the General Education Diploma test, to find a job to support the child. Because of the stigmatism she encountered in the local community and at home, she again had to decide to marry at age sixteen. While her friends where going out on dates and high school parties, she was at home, pretending to be a wife and mother, which she knew nothing about. By the age seventeen, she became very depressed and withdrawn; this depression would last for over twenty years.

According to Lee (2013) family and peers support influences the psychological well-being of teenage mothers. Support from friends and relatives, in particularly female siblings, and male partners contributes a key role in levels of stress in a pregnant teen's life. I had neither.

Poverty in the Black Church and Communities

Race and education are also important in explaining variations in psychological well-being of teenage mothers (Lee, 2013). According to Lee (2013) in order for mothers to make the transition from being a youth to a parent requires resources, which may be limited for young mothers. Traditionally, pregnant adolescents have been considered a risk group for depressive symptoms and inferior quality of life (Pires, Araújo-Pedrosa, Canavarro, 2014). Transitioning from an adolescent to a parent in nine months is off-time. Research has shown that teen pregnancy is a potential cognitive predictor of maladjustment during pregnancy (Pires et al., 2014). Adolescents have a more negative perception of the impact of pregnancy in body image, family and romantic relationships, school, work, and emotions.

God's image is imprinted in all mankind, giving inherent dignity for all those who are existing in poverty. Therefore, this book will provide distinctly biblical, theological, reflections and examples from United States history. This book will formulate an ethical framework for social change and social action. I will have utilized quotes from Theologian James Cone to further corroborate that without cooperation from Black leaders and systems that consist of interdependent parts when combined to make an organized whole of eliminating poverty, the cycle of poverty in the Black church and community will continue.

Leaders need solid reasons for eliminating poverty in the Black church and community. Some reasons include generational poverty and limited representation to the population at large. Social justice and equality are becoming out of reach for this population in the world's most affluent country. Social injustice and inequality must be exposed. The current rate of poverty in the Black church and communities will ultimately lead to economic and social chaos, unless due diligence is incorporated into the system of social change.

Social change is social action, which will ultimately lead to change towards social and economic justice in the Black church and Black communities. Social action must take place to measure the elimination of poverty in the Black communities. Leaders will need to make efforts to modify societal institutions to meet needs, resolve issues, achieve social and economic justice, and provide for the well-being of the church and community members.

Social action is also a vital part of the system for change. This system involves advocacy, which entails fighting for the rights of low-income or no-income individuals and families who do not have a voice in society. There needs to be a social movement on the part of Spiritual leaders; this needs to transpire on a large scale to effect economic and social justice for the underprivilege and underserved.

White Christians promote their superiority to other nations and religions (Adams et al., 2013) via racism and discrimination. White Christians used this religion to promote and induce suppression and oppression of Native Americans, African Americans, Jews, and others. They obtain this using force, violence, harassment, and discrimination (Adams et al., 2013).

Racism and Christianity is synonymous to White supremacy. Christianity has been used as a front since the early settlers came over from Europe. White Christians utilized their religion to slaughter Native Americans, enslave African Americans and harass and torment "Others'" religions (Adams et al, 2013). Some White Christians attempt to diminish or destroy the worth and dignity of the "others" (Adams et al., 2013). Recognition and respect for the lower class regardless of their race is normally nonexistent by the White Christian. Most White Christians will not attend the same church as African Americans, Mexicans, or Natives.

James Cone writes:
"The Christian community, therefore, is that community that freely becomes oppressed, because they know that Jesus himself has defined humanity's liberation in the context of

what happens to the little ones. Christians join the cause of the oppressed in the fight for justice not because of some philosophical principle of 'the Good' or because of a religious feeling of sympathy for people in prison. Sympathy does not change the structures of injustice. The authentic identity of Christians with the poor is found in the claim which the Jesus-encounter lays upon their own lifestyle, a claim that connects the word 'Christian' with the liberation of the poor. Christians fight not for humanity in general but for themselves and out of their love for concrete human beings."

Human beings display God's image with dignity, purpose, value, and therefore, deserves economic and social justice. God has given all mankind exclusive dignity, value, and purpose as the apple of His eye. Despite the fall, man continues to be God's forgiven people and deserves mercy, justice, and equity in these United States of America. The gospel becomes central to any injustice, discrimination, and racism. Although the Black American culture comprises Christianity, Black Americans are amongst the poorest in the nation. (Adams et al, 2013).

James Cone (2013) asserts that White supremacy is the American Church's prevailing, and most persistent immorality. Spiritual leaders in the church and community have claimed that there is one church under the divine inspiration of God, but on Sunday morning the church exercises extreme racism and separation. Until all people come together under one God, Black churches and communities will remain in poverty, oppression, and marginalization. To heighten the viewpoint, an analogy of a movie of an integrated family will be penned.

The Blind Side

The Blind Side is a true story referencing Michael Oher. Michael was one of his mother's twelve or more children. Michael's mother was portrayed as crack addicted. All of Michael's siblings had been removed from the mothers' care due to her addiction. Michael grew up in foster care as a small child. As a teenager Michael had run away from his recent foster home and was living with a family that took him in temporarily. Michael was riding with a friend and his father to a private Christian school, when the father suggested to Coach Cook to consider enrolling Michael in the Christian school as well. Coach Cook was impressed by Michael's size and talents; as a result, Michael could attend the school.

Michael was a very humble and quiet person. S.J. Tuohy was the youngest child of the Tuohy family. S.J. attended the Christian school. S.J. became friends with Michael. The friendship lead to S.J.'s parents taking an interest in Michael. Michael was homeless currently; he did not have any money, clothes, or food. Mr. Sean Tuohy noticed that after a game one night, Michael was scrounging around the gym for leftover food. One chilly night the Tuohy family noticed Michael walking to the gym. The Tuohy family picked Michael up that night and took him to their eloquent home.

The next morning as Michael was leaving the Tuohy home; Mrs. Tuohy stopped him and invited him to stay for Thanksgiving dinner. The children accepted Michael into the home, despite him being a very large African American male. The Tuohy's were a Caucasian family. Mrs. Tuohy offered Michael a room in their home. Michael became a part of the Tuohy's family in a brief time.

The most important demographic social problem covered in the movie is the fact that Michael is African American. The Tuohy family were upper-class Caucasians. Although the Tuohy family readily accepted Michael, friends and family did not. Mrs. Tuohy's social group was suspicious of Michael living in the Tuohy's home with their Caucasian daughter. One friend suggested that Mrs. Tuohy may have been experiencing guilt for being Caucasian and privileged. Another friend asked Mrs. Tuohy, what her dead father would think of an African American living in their home.

The social problem that is affecting Michael Oher and the Tuohy family is interracial living. Interracial living is defined as a family or couple of different race living in the same home. Even after decades of seeing interracial couples and families, the subject is still seen as taboo in some American cities, especially in the south. Even with this great divide among races, interracial living across the nation has steadily grown. The hope of American citizens to turn a blind eye to racism lies in the famous speech given by Dr. Martin Luther King's, "I have a dream." Dr. King's dream was to one day live in a nation where individuals would not be judged by the color of their skin, but by the content of their character.

The Tuohy family did not receive much support from the outside community. There was opposition from family, friends, and the NAACP. When Mrs. Tuohy and Michael returned to Michael's old neighborhood, they were faced with opposition and danger. Mrs. Tuohy visited the local Department of Family and Children Service. Here she did not face the same kind of racism and opposition. Governmental entities, such as, foster care and adoption agencies support interracial living. Some churches also support interracial living.

A challenge for spiritual leaders, dealing with interracial living perpetuates from the micro, macro, and mezzo perspective. The social policy addressed in the film, can be at its best, racism. Spiritual leaders must intervene in the individual adaption to the living arrangement, as well as the communities' response to the family. It is believed that the church must introduce these type families to a diversified social network that is able to transition them into a stable living environment.

The Touhy family was indeed color blind. The family accepted Michael as a respectful human being, regardless of being African American. Eventually, the teachers and other administration of the school respected Michael for his ability to learn and achieve his goal to play football. Although the NACCP and some school officials suspected that the Tuohy family had an ulterior motive for bringing Michael into their family, it was later proven that the family's motive was love and respect.

Michael was able to accomplish an education, love, respect, and a career because of being taken into a Caucasian upper-class family. These opportunities would not have been afforded to him had he remained in his impoverished neighborhood in Hurt village. If Michael had remained in foster care, it is likely that he would not have bonded with the foster family. When Michael returned to his old neighborhood, he learned that nothing had changed. His old friend had dropped out of school and joined a gang. Michael's friend was later killed.

The film did not focus on social or economic justice for a race of people, but on one individual, whom the Tuohy's found favor in. The Tuohy's were a wealthy family; this allowed them to easily transition Michael into their family, community and school. People that lived in Hurt village were portrayed as being dangerous. The upper-class citizens of the Tuohy's community had never heard of Hurt village. Mrs. Tuohy admitted she had lived in Memphis, Tennessee all her life and had never been to the area where Michael grew up.

This film was very inspirational. The idea of the Tuohy family bringing a large African American male into their lavish home and upper-class community was surprising. It was suspected that from the beginning the parents may have known that Michael had enormous potential to become a famous NFL player. It also believed that the family would have taken him in even if Michael did not have this potential. Michael may not have remained in the home if he did not have such a humble, childlike character. Michael's ability to be a productive athlete contributed to him being allowed in the predominately white Christian school. Michael played a very important role in channeling his own future.

Interracial families urgently need more support from the church community. The courage of the Tuohy family to go against the norm and have an African American male in their home is to be commended.

James Cone writes:
And certainly, the history of the black-white relations in this country from the Civil War to the present unmistakably show that as a people, America has never intended for blacks to be

free. To this day, in the eyes of most white Americans, the black man remains subhuman.

There have been several leaders attempting to rectify poverty in the Black community and church. Josephine Shaw Lowell (1843-1905), a social reformer, was one of these leaders. Mrs. Lowell is the founder of the New York City Charity Organization Society. She was a vivid advocate of social charities. Ms. Lowell believed that charity should offer more than temporary relief from poverty, and that charity should also motivate and enhance the individual towards a more sustainable life (Hansan, 2013).

Josephine Shaw Lowell

$\mathcal{M}$rs. Lowell's was educated in several states, such as New York, Rome, Paris, and Boston. These were the years of her education. During these early years, she displayed an ardent desire to help others. Her mother worked with the Woman's Central Relief Association in New York City, assisting soldiers. Josephine joined her mother in taking care of the soldiers and quickly realized that she had an innate desire to work with people (Hansan, 2013).

Josephine became a volunteer during the Civil War and continued to organized charities throughout the duration of her life (Hansan, 2013). The following are examples of the charities and organizations she founded or offered her faithful services: American Red Cross, Women's Central Association of Relief, New York Charity Organization Society (founder), and House of Refuge for Women" (Hansan, 2013). These are a few of the many contributions Mrs. Lowell has dedicated to the path and development of the social work arena.

It is difficult to distinguish which of the many charities and organizations that Mrs. Lowell established is the most significant. This martyr of social justice dedicated a lifetime of work to this field. Because of the birth of this organization, other charitable agencies were established. Josephine worked wholeheartedly for twenty-five years with New York Charity Organization Society, serving in many capacities. Mrs. Lowell served until her death in 1905 (Hansan, 2013).

The example of Josephine Lowell is kindred to what is needed again today in the Black community and church. In researching her many accomplishments, achievements, and establishments, I was inspired by her endless effort to make contributions into the lives of all people in society. A leader must create opportunities where opportunities do not exist. Mrs. Lowell created charities, social services, and trailblazing change as the first female commissioner of the New York State Board of Charities (Hansan, 2013).

Josephine Lowell represented social justice, equal rights, equal opportunities, for those who are often overlooked. She was a voice for those who do not have a voice. It is informative and inspiring to learn that Mrs. Lowell, being a wealthy Caucasian, dedicated a lifetime of assisting people that were not a part of her social status. She was a proficient and productive advocate for the less fortunate. Her attributes are inspiring and motivating. A leader's responsibility is to represent, advocate, motivate, and create opportunities for those who cannot do this for themselves regardless of the leader's race. Mrs. Lowell accomplished this through perseverance and determination.

Poverty Exists in Black Ideology

During the early 1960s the social change temperament took on new and exciting efforts. One of these efforts came in the form of the civil rights movement. This movement was accompanied by other movements that challenged entitlements, racial equality, and local control of community institutions. This was the era of Lyndon Johnson's presidency. The presidency declared a war on poverty and created many programs to combat existing and ongoing poverty. This was a time that Black leaders confronted racism and sexism. The various leaders met with organized groups with many agendas, but a unified goal, to declare war on social and economic injustice. Unfortunately, during the conservative era of the 1980s, public funding that had been allocate for poverty in African American communities were eradicated. Poverty for the Black church and its constituents is structured into our society on so many levels, and in so many ways. This is a product of our capitalistic system, creating the haves and the have-nots. It is reflected in our varying socioeconomic classes and the ever-widening gap between the wealthy and the poor, the wealthy and the middle-class (Rogers, 2013). Poverty is something that people are born into, or not born into. It is glossed over by familiar phrases like "pull oneself up by their boot straps," "all men are created equal," and "land of opportunity."

Poverty exists in our ideology, our institutions, and on an individual level. It affects people's opportunities by creating an unequal starting point for one's life. Changes need to occur, on some level, in all systems at the micro, mezzo, and macro levels (Rogers, 2013).

According to Zastrow & Kirst-Ashman (2016) Maslow's hierarchy of needs, people will consistently work towards their needs to maintain stability and daily functioning. When someone is struggling to make ends meet because they have a low-paying job or experiencing stress on a regular basis due to any of the "isms," it's harder to take advantage of opportunities to make positive change in one's life—if those opportunities are even readily available. Making change is difficult because it's a multifaceted problem.

During the days of Moses, we see that God established some guidelines under the law to help the poor. The word of God tells the Israelites to help the aliens, widows, orphans, and the poor. God protects their property, warns again against showing favoritism, and sets up a system of "gleaning" to help prevent starvation and malnourishment (Ex. 23:10-12 King James Version).

Poverty is structured in our society through many "isms," which are strengthened through assumptions, social learning theory, and conflicts in one's environment. Whether inequality is proliferated due to your race, gender, sexuality, age, or class doesn't matter (Zastrow & Kirst-Ashman 2016).

A leader's responsibility lies in "best practices" ways to increase organizational accountability, to a larger spectrum of all individual interests. Spiritual leaders could impact poverty-stricken individuals by becoming familiar with the Socio-Cultural Perspective. This theory encompasses a long-standing question about equal representation. Socio-Cultural measures social inequality in nature. Human experience of inequalities is strongly grounded in cultural process (Rogers 2013). Cultural processes are revealed in the form of organizations and institutions in which individuals live (Rogers 2013).

Rogers (2013) suggests that organizations and societies coexist and co-influence each other. Society level cultural processes influence organizational processes and vice-versa, which results in social and economic inequality. The problematic aspects of this theory are when a leader does not educate oneself on the cultural belief of individuals, he inhibits the ability to successfully affect change in the realm of influence. Assuming all people are the same is a myth. Leaders must realize that individuals are both recipients and shapers of culture (Rogers, 2013).

Spiritual leaders must address these issues on a micro, mezzo, and macro level. According to Adams et al, (2013) any form that offers a specific group of people privileges because of their race, sex, religion, or social status is discrimination. Throughout history, many Christian missionary efforts and enterprises have focused on inequalities. Equality is a means to spreading the gospel to those who need empowerment. This focus is especially true to the poor and the indigent (Adams et al., 2013).

African Americans are harassed and tormented as "Others" religions (Adams et al, 2013).

Nationally, leaders must advocate for the enforcement of the United Nations Universal Declaration of Human Rights (Adams et al., 2013). Regardless of where racism derived from, every human in the world deserves the same health care, rights, respect, dignity as anyone else. Spiritual leaders must be on the right side of history (Adams et al., 2013).

Becoming an ally, as a leader will affect those in the present and in the future. Spiritual leaders must speak out against injustice of any form, to include religious injustice. Spiritual leaders must advocate for human equality in local, state, and federal government (Adams et al., 2013). "If one of your countrymen becomes poor and is unable to support himself among you, help him as you would an alien or a temporary resident, so he can continue to live among you. Do not take interest of any kind from him, but fear your God, so that your countrymen may continue to live among you…." — Leviticus 25:35-36 (NIV)

James Cone writes:
"If the Church is to remain faithful to its Lord, it must make a decisive break with the structure of this society by launching a vehement attack on the evils of racism in all forms. It must become prophetic, demanding a radical change in the interlocking structures of this society.

Models of Intervention

The three models of intervention that are needed in the Black church and community are, "Black Identity Development, The Four 'Is' of Oppression and Social Change Model" all have the same aim regardless of how it is accomplished, and this is to improve and maintain the conditions which affect the lives of the communities and Black churches. Improving social and emotional development is important to spiritual leaders because the general concept of being a leader is to advocate for change and to empower parishioners.

The four "Is" of oppression model is used to teach individuals in the community to be informed of oppression on the individual level, institutional level, interpersonal level, and the ideology of oppression. Individuals buy into the ideology of oppression that degrades minorities' values, beliefs and rights (Adams et.al, 2005). Individuals are socialized to accept systems of oppression as norms. The plan proposal includes teachings of how communities can interrupt negative socialization by stepping out of the cycle of oppression and encompassing new awareness, information and action (Adams et.al, 2010).

Social change is the act of breaking free of existing systems and affects a shift to a new system. (Ichiro, 2015) implies social change is a struggle between pro-change and pro-establishment powers. To increase the probability of true social change, action that will lead to social and economic justice must transpire. This book addresses the potential impact of white privilege on African Americans from both dominant and minority groups and how intersecting identities might impact an individual's experience. How a spiritual leader utilizes cultural strengths when working with African Americans is a relevant factor towards social change.

There are many skills a spiritual leader may use to engage in anti-oppressive work; the person-in-environment perspective is an approach in understanding the relationship between person and social environment. Although the individual is viewed as separate from social systems that transact with each other in relationships of similar influences. The individual and the social systems co-constitute their environment (Kondrat, 2002). Kondrat (2002) explains micro-macro relationship and the person-in-environment perspective through utilizing critical theory.

Duba (2005) has defined the biopsychosocial model as a "new therapeutic system." This model surpasses the individual's system or issues and considers social factors and the way these factors interact with biological, psychological and social issues. The biopsychosocial model encompasses three domains, the biological, the psychological, and the social; therefore, requiring multiple treatment interventions.

Poverty among African Americans exists on the micro, macro, and mezzo levels. Leaders should use theories that are deemed appropriate to assist the church and community on each level. There is more than one theory to utilize in combating poverty in the African American community. The interventions developed from each theory reflect the need and concerns of each case. The spiritual leaders must become active in formulating the goals and interventions for the church and community by verbalizing the status of poverty and oppression.

Krantz & Williams (2013) proposes that, "biological, psychological, social, and structural processes operate in a matrix of nested and inextricably connected subsystems that influence all aspects of mental and physical health." Yet it is also believed that African Americans have been traumatized due to the intensity of racism and oppression. This has contributed to the stagnation of the Black church and community. It is believed that this group of people have lost their identity, from being, Colored, Negros, Black, to African Americans.

According to Robert Cross (1991) Black individuals are not comfortable with displaying their culture or beliefs in the United States of America. Blacks have been shamed because of the darkness of their skin and their lack of socialization and education. Cross interpreted this fallacy as accepted by Black Americans, especially the church, due to its promotion by White Americans. Cross believed that Black Americans were in an identity crisis. He wrote on the Nigrescence theory in 1991. This theory explained that Black individuals needed a re-socializing experience that would transforms a preexisting identity (e.g., non-Afrocentric identity) to one that is Afrocentric.

Hence; Cross introduced a five-stage Nigrescence model in 1971, but in 1991 he condensed it to four stages combining stages four and five. I reviewed the original five stages.

> Cross writes:
> Pre-encounter (stage 1) depicts the identity to be changed; Encounter (stage 2) isolates the point at which the person feels compelled to change; Immersion Emersion (stage 3) describes the vortex of identity change; and Internalization and Internalization-Commitment (stages 4 and 5) describe the habituation and internalization of the new identity.

In the Pre-encounter stage, Blacks are in denial of their culture and image. They prefer to identify with the White culture that has been imbedded in them as being the best. In this stage Blacks focus on surviving from day to day and preoccupy themselves with occupation, lifestyle, and religion as more relevant. Blacks at this stage, deny that race has negatively affected their lives. Some Black people may accept their Blackness while others may have an attitude of anti-Blackness.

In the pre-encounter stage, leaders are needed to express that Blacks should not feel alienated from their culture or image but embrace it as beauty and strength. The Black church and community should be utilized as potential or actual sources of personal support and strength. Most African Americans fail to realize that they have been raised with White westernized ideologies, because it is so embedded in their culture.

According to Cross (1991) the encounter stage incorporates two steps, encounter and personalize. Normally something must transpire in the individual's life that will transform the way he interprets and receive his race. In personalizing a Black individual began to act on his new views of his Black culture and inheritance. This experience helps to navigate the person towards Nigrescence. The experience serves as a stimulus to evoke change in their thinking. Leaders in the encounter stage must labor, toil, or avert the belief that Blackness is bad or negative. They must give guidance to the congregation and communities which thrust the person into re-socializing or transforming into a positive sense of Blackness.

The immersion-emersion stage of Nigrescence is the desired outcome of Cross's theory. Until Black people embrace who they are as a people, Black identity will be evaded. This is the stage of psychological, sociological, and ecologically credence (Cross, 1991). At this stage Black people start to discard the old stereotype that Black is bad, and White is right theory. The old world-view of adapting to White culture is purged and a new mindset is developed. The person is contemplating change and moving towards Nigrescence. Cross (1991) contends that immersion is a pervasive ideology that is consistently motivated by anger towards Caucasians that forced them to accept Blackness as subordinated to Whiteness.

This motivation is negative entropy of the immersion-emersion stage and can be a catalyst for Black spiritual leaders to invest in their congregates and community's teachings on the Black history, art, and music that represent a culture they have been ignorant of. According to Vandiver et al., (2001), Black people can feel a variety of different emotions expressed in diverse ways. If Blacks accepted being Black then, they were assumed to be psychologically healthy and to have a high self-esteem. In contrast Blacks who accepted the values of White society were believed to suffer from self-hatred and, as a result, low self-esteem. Unless our Black leaders advocate for social change that will produce societal reconstructions that ensures disadvantaged Black people have access to live as Americans and love themselves as American, self-hatred among the Black race may continue to prevail. Individuals during the immersion stage, began to view themselves from a unique perspective. The negative stereotypes that were once dominant in influencing self-worth with Blackness, takes a back seat.

"During this stage the person transcend through personal growth and the recognition that certain role models or heroes operate from a more advance state of identity development" (Cross, 1991). Internalization-commitment focuses on the long-term interest of Black affairs over an extended amount of time (Cross, 1991). This stage is now combined. According to Benjamin et al. (1998), the Black identity development model helps "Blacks begin to shed a poor self-worth and move toward embracing a positive Black self-definition" (p. 96).

Transformation takes place during this stage. The individuals go through each stage of the Black identity process concurrently. Black people are not always knowledgeable of their Black identity from a positive perspective, as they` progress and become informed of the affirmative of being Black, the individuals develop nigrescence.

The Black person then feels liberated to become active in making a difference in their churches and communities. The person seeks to advocate for the marginalized and oppressed Black church and community. This is the stage that the Black person is aware of the reality of institutional racism, discrimination, oppression and marginalization. Utilizing Cross's (1991) Nigrescence theory is instrumental in enlightening the Black church and community pertaining to many reasons for ongoing poverty in the Black church. Due to this race of people being taught to think of themselves as inferior, inadequate, and less than human, is the stigma that retains the status quo of poverty in the Black church and community.

Enabling the Black community to remain in poverty and suppression has been a longstanding agenda of the White oppressor. Normally handicapping individuals by discriminating against them works well as a means of keeping that person in a position of limitations. The Black church and community remains stagnant and immobile in facilitating empowerment seminars or services. The gospel is sometimes used to criticize the Black person for wanting to live a better life, the scripture that is used, quotes that "It is easier for a rich man to get through the eye of a needle than to enter into heaven" (Matthew: 19-24). This is taught to uneducated Black Americans to comfort them in their present state of poverty. Nevertheless, the Black leaders sometime evade scripture, which teaches that God desires for his people to prosper, even as their soul prospers. It is imperative for the Spiritual leaders in the Black community to begin to educate and motivate congregates to move from a place of complacency to a place of nigrecence.

This is to say White privileges have been afforded to the dominant group for many years. This group has utilized these privileges to excel in economy, education, social, and institutions (Adams et al., 67, 2013). The dominate group experiences major and minor privileges that entail an extensive list. According to Adams et al., (2013) there is a cost of racism. The American economy has suffered due to institutional racism. The price is not as high for the minority group as the dominant group, yet everyone is affected negatively due to racism. One example is productivity is reduced in the workplace if racism is practiced. The housing industry is staggered due to minorities being discriminated against by banks and loan companies (Adams et al., 2013).

Additionally, data supports the facts that individuals living in oppressed neighborhoods are more likely to be susceptible to racial injustice. Individuals living in these neighborhoods are challenged with a higher risk of teen pregnancy, drug use and criminal activity. The transition to individual and community development requires significant readjustment in lifestyle, resources, and relationships that often pressures emotional well-being. The dominant group in society does not face these challenges at the same level due to White privileges.

> James Cone Writes:
> "Black Power, in short, is an attitude, an inward affirmation of the essential worth of blackness. It means that the black man will not be poisoned by the stereotypes that others have of him, but will affirm from the depth of his soul: 'Get used to me, I am not getting used to anyone.'" 16 And "'if the white man challenges my humanity, I will impose my whole weight as a man on his life and show him that I am not that 'sho good eatin' that he persists in imagining."
> James H. Cone, Black Theology and Black Power

It is believed that in a society where resources are plentiful, and opportunity is available, United State Citizens should not suffer the poverty that is being witnessed. Poverty is perhaps America's greatest embarrassment. It is hard to believe that people are so deep in poverty, in a country with such a bevy of resources, wealth, and historically unprecedented amount of riches, power, and potential. The American experience of the poor is so different from the experience of the "haves" that they might as well be in a different country. But they are not.

My Story Part Two

History supports the facts that as a poor African American female, I was challenged with a higher risk of teen pregnancy. For adult mothers the transition to motherhood requires significant readjustment in lifestyle, resources, and relationships that often pressures emotional well-being. For teenage mothers the transition is more complicated by the normal developmental task of adolescence. For example, the young mother's dependency on her caregivers for support of parenting, training, and preparation for parenthood inhibits the development of feelings of independence, an important task in adolescence (Pires et al., 2014).

As a young mother, I was a part of an unstable family life, low cognitive skills, and feelings of deprivation and dependency. I was also immature, insecure, and had a feeling of hopelessness, low self-esteem, and low self-worth. I believe that the successful transition of a teenage mother depends on the socioeconomic and cultural environment in which pregnancy occurs. As an experienced teen mother, I believe that my family system influenced my decision to engage in sexual intercourse at an early age; I have discussed this fact using the social learning theory.

As far as progressing through the developmental stages of growth, I did not transition through this process in a healthy manner. At the time I should have been confirming my identity, I had another human identity growing inside of me. This was indeed a conflict. During the time I should have been thinking about my future and what I wanted to do with my life, I had to consider the life that I had given birth to.

Because of being part of an impoverished family and environment, I had very little to offer my child. Because of witnessing all the lack and injustice around me, I decided as a child that the child that I had given life to would not inherit the curse of poverty from me. I became self-motivated, by the age of twenty-five; I received my Bachelors of Social Work, followed by a master's degree in counseling. I became a Certified Addiction Counselor in the State of Georgia, achieved a Doctorate Degree in Counseling, Master of Social Work and finally, License Master Social Worker. In 2004, I was ordained as a Pastor and Spiritual leader.

Teenage pregnancy is an off-time event that entails many factors, but it is not a sentence or excuse for failure. Today there are many programs offered to teenage mothers and fathers to support them as young parents. There are many tools and resources available to teen parents, such as, free daycare assistant, financial support, and health care.

As a teen, I made a poor decision to engage in sexual intercourse. The result was pregnancy. As a young adult, I made a wise decision to become educated and responsible for the child that I gave birth to. Teen pregnancy is an off-time transition, but with perseverance and determination life can get back on course.

> "Indeed, our survival and liberation depend upon our recognition of the truth when it is spoken and lived by the people. If we cannot recognize the truth, then it cannot liberate us from untruth. To know the truth is to appropriate it, for it is not mainly reflection and theory. Truth is divine action entering our lives and creating the human action of liberation."
>
> - James H. Cone

It can be asserted that Spiritual leaders serve as representatives of the Black church, its mission, and its core values. They know the church's history. Spiritual leaders commit themselves to the church's enhancement and to their own spiritual conduct and growth. Spiritual leaders advocate for individual access to the services in the communities; practice personal reflection and self-correction to assure continual spiritual development; attend to church roles and boundaries; demonstrate spiritual demeanor in behavior, appearance, and communication; engage in career-long learning; and use supervision and consultation. This is just the beginning of what service to the church means.

As Spiritual leaders one is expected to provide services to help congregate function in society and are also required to put effort into social justice and practice awareness concerning integrity and competence. Expectations are highly placed on spiritual leaders displaying dignity worth and understanding the value of human relationship. One of the main purposes of spiritual leaders are providing service.

Spiritual leaders are very important to everyday life. They are the ones that help people in need when they have nobody else to turn to. Also, they provide resources and better understanding of predicaments that individuals could be experiencing. There are so many ways a spiritual leader can help members and communities deal with their problems and come up with a solution. It is up to that leader and individual or group to identify the problem and see what theory fits.

Each person, regardless of position in society, has basic human rights, such as freedom, safety, privacy, an adequate standard of living, health care, and education. Spiritual leaders recognize the global interconnections of oppression and are knowledgeable about theories of justice and strategies to promote human and civil rights. Spiritual leadership incorporates social justice practices in organizations, institutions, and society to ensure that these basic human rights are distributed equitably and without prejudice. Spiritual leaders understand the forms and mechanisms of oppression and discrimination; advocate for human rights and social and economic justice; and engage in practices that advance social and economic justice.

A code of responsibility and leadership is simply a belief system in which one does some things because they are "good," and avoids doing other things because they are "bad." Formal law has very little to do with a personal code of ethics. One develops and is responsible for this by themself, though parents and social contacts have a lot to do with it. Here is an example: there are very few places in which a bystander has any legal obligation to come to the aid of a third party. And yet, people help others all the time—because it is the "right" thing to do in their belief systems.

Honesty, integrity, loyalty, and respect are highly valued, and these values are present in everyday life. The following briefly describes the core ideals that should be maintained: honesty —it is firmly believed that honesty is the best policy. It will have to be an extreme situation that involves severe injury; damage or other loss that will convince me that not being truthful is best. It is realized that the truth can often be very painful, can cause anger, distrust, and hatred; but, if truthful information and guidance has been given to oppressed individuals, they will possibly hold me in a higher regard. This honesty will hopefully allow a greater trust between leaders and community members and future dealings will be less likely to be strained.

The outside barrier that makes it difficult to confront racism is the old systems that have been in place for many years. Some systems may be reluctant to any type of modification or change (Griffith et al., 2007). The amount of time and effort that it will take to confront racism on a macro level may be an inward barrier. I am a full-time pastor and a full-time therapist; these responsibilities leave me with very limited time to take on new tasks. The outside resources that will assist me in confronting racism are polices that have been implemented that make racism/discrimination illegal, such as, fair housing, equal employment opportunities, and voting rights. My innate ability to empathize with others that are less fortunate than I am will assist me in confronting racism/discrimination.

The steps that I will continue to take to confront and overcome racism will remain to maintain a strong personal faith in God. Secondly, I plan to become more involved in advocating for social change. I plan to do this by being involved in local and state committees. I will keep informed of new social policies and the status and implementation of these policies. Thirdly, I will continue to encourage minorities to exercise their right to vote for local, state, and federal officials. Finally, I will continue working with clergywomen on social concerns.

Spiritual leaders may approach the matter of faith as just a series of religious exercises without substance. Most members focus on rituals and traditions. Leadership sometimes seems reduced to rules and regulations, or forms and appearances. But, in fact, the Bible presents a faith that is real and powerful, based on a real relationship with the living God! It is a faith that changes lives, socially, emotionally, and economically. There is supremacy to be a spiritual leader, who also displays excellent faith, and gives life meaning! This power was important to the life of Jesus who went about "healing all who were oppressed by the devil" (Acts 10:38). This same power was given to His followers when the Holy Spirit came upon them (Acts 1:8).

The Black church nor its community is so broken and messed up that God cannot put it back together again. There is not a church or community that is too far off from God that He can't reach down and turn the tables.

David went through a series of difficulties during his lifetime. At times, torrents of problems swept over him, threatening to overwhelm him like a raging flood. He faced giants and hostile armies. He had to flee for his life and seek refuge among people who once were his enemies. He experienced the rejection and doubts of his family. And the king whom he had served faithfully turned against him and sought to kill him.

God did not prevent him from going through these situations. However, God always was with him, and David recognized that God made the difference in his life. Without God he would have drowned in the waters and been torn apart by his adversaries. He would have been trapped just like a bird in the snare of the trapper. But, because of God, the snare was broken. Sometimes, when spiritual leaders experience problems, they can be surprised, or feel discouraged, defeated, or overwhelmed. But, like David, Spiritual leaders need to realize that they are not immune from problems just because they believe in God or seek to serve Him. But leaders can know that He always is with us. That He will bring them through difficulties and give strength that is needed.

Today, remember that God is with you in every situation that you face. You can look to Him to bring you through, protect you, shield you, guide you, and provide for you. Call on Him for the things you need, and trust in Him. Be at peace and remember: He is on your side. If you have a relationship with God, He is on your side.

Spiritual leaders, although chosen by God to be His front-runners, are far from perfect. Redeemed, yes, but righteous, no! If we're honest with ourselves, we might very well conclude that we share many imperfect characteristics. The secret is, in every circumstance, in every instance of weakness, we must learn to cast the Cross of Christ into those experiences and allow the sacrifice of the precious blood of Jesus to cleanse, deliver, and strengthen us. We must learn to trust in Jesus and in nothing else.

Submission to discipline isn't easy. The natural reaction is to become resentful or even rebellious when life takes a hard turn. The spiritual way is to have an attitude of submission to God's will and practice perseverance. All too often people will leave the church, abandon God, and look to other means of comfort as though it is God's fault that they fail or the church's fault for not helping them more.

Spiritual leaders must look beyond the circumstances and endure to the sovereign God, whose mind and heart control all affairs. It's not a matter of resentfully resigning ourselves to our lot, but rather to be in willing subjection to our Heavenly Father, refusing to let opposition get us down. The Cross of Christ will make your life's lemons into lemonade. The Cross of Christ will turn your bitterness into sweetness. The Cross of Christ will turn your disillusionment into a new vision. The blood of Jesus will lift you out of the miry clay and set your feet on the rock to stay. Bring your weariness to Jesus and let Him make it sweet today.

After writing this book, I realized that initially I felt overwhelmed about having to revisit old wounds that racism and hearing stories from older relatives had inflicted upon me. I understand now that those wounds needed to be healed and life must go on. I was really elated that I have been able to keep some of the feelings and responses suppressed for so long. I feel to write about these injustices, has started a healing process. My experience with racism can never change, but my attitude towards the ignorance of racism has changed; therefore, my response would change to reflect more knowledge and understanding of systematic and institutionalized racism. As I reviewed this writing, I felt relieved to share some of the old feelings that I now realized are no longer relevant to my life. I am better equipped to deal with the reality of racism without allowing it to become personal. I learned several things about myself while researching; first I understand that I no longer suppress old feelings against individuals that have discriminated against me because of my race.

Secondly, I learned that it did not matter as much to me if someone disliked or attempted to discriminate against me because of my race. I understand now that the issue is not with me personally, but with the individual. I understand that my impressions toward racism and discrimination may have been limited to my environment and to what I have been taught. I had not viewed racism from a macro or mezzo level. I had not understood racism as a part of a system or institution. My responses were strictly from my subjective experiences and feelings. The model that I utilize where I am now, being the Black Identity Development Model. Immediately after reading the five stages of the Black Identity Development Model, I was able to confirm that I was experiencing the fourth stage, which is, internalization (Sue, 2006.) The Cross model describes this stage as being characterized by inner security, as conflicts between the old and new identities are resolved (Cross, 1995). One event that has facilitated the change in my development of racial identity, is simply being in a neighborhood with Caucasians, African Americans and other races of people who share their experiences or lack of experience with other races. I have spoken with Caucasian neighbors that share that they have been reared in an all Caucasian neighborhood or school. These individuals have minimal knowledge of the impact that racism has had on African Americans. I believe that most of my Caucasian neighbors have never thought much about racism or white privileges, to no fault of their own, but were never challenged to do so.

Another experience—I had recently engaged in a conversation with my neighbor, who is an older Caucasian male. My neighbor shared some subjective experiences he has had in fighting for minorities and others who he felt did not have a voice. I had never taken the initiative to have a conversation with him, just wave hello and keep going. Since being in the neighborhood, I took the time to have a conversation with him, which was very pleasant. My neighbor has no control over how others of his race think or act. I realized that he is one of the nicest and caring people I know.

The last stage of Black identity that Cross identified in his model is internalization-commitment. This stage expresses a commitment that the individual has toward social change, social justice, and civil rights. In this stage the individual does not just speak of social change but acts to contribute towards social change (Cross, 1995).

Personal concerns that I have resolved are being able to express my feelings on racism, verses suppressing these feelings and not speaking about them. I have been apprehensive in the past on speaking about racism because I felt it would conjure up old feelings that are not pleasant. I feel that I can discuss racism and discrimination without letting the subject affect me personally. Religion is the factor that has sustained me throughout my life. There have been times in my life when I wanted to treat those who I felt have treated me unfairly the same way.

Because of my Spiritual teaching and faith, I have been able to overcome that temptation. Religion has been central to my sense of self because I have been able to see myself in the way that I believe God views me. My racial identity story began when I was fourteen. Erickson's theory identifies stage five as being the adolescence identity versus identity confusion (Rogers, 2013). During this time of growth, a teenager is discovering who they are. Teenagers are determining self-identity. Some teenagers have a tough time integrating their roles into their identity; this causes confusion (Rogers, 2013).

As a poor fourteen-year-old African American female, I was identifying with my environment. My environment was composed of African American teenage girls who were trying to find their identity in securing affirmation from a male. The result for most of us was becoming pregnant during this time of transition, which magnified the confusion. As a fourteen-year old African American female, I was afraid and confused. I felt hopeless for myself and the child that I carried. I realized that I had made an extremely poor choice or allowed myself to be in a position of compromise. During this time, 1970s male dominance was more prevalent, so surrendering to pressure from a male was normal. Teenage pregnancy was a result of my poor socioeconomic status (Brien, Loya, and Pepper, 2002).

My story has not changed, but my knowledge of factors evolving around my racial identity has changed. I am now more knowledgeable of the systems that I was a part of that contributed to my racial identification. Because of my poor economic status and lack of family support, I made poor decisions that reflect my African American environment. My knowledge of racial identity will never be the same. I feel that I am more empowered as a person versus being empowered as an African American female.

Conclusion

The inspiration of this book comes from Maya Angelou's autobiography, *I Know Why the Caged Bird Sings*. In her autobiography, Angelou revealed that as a young girl she had been raped by her mother's boyfriend. The traumatic act caused Angelo to go into a deep depression and isolation. She refused to speak for years. Even when Angelou was placed in a safe home with her grandmother, she was afraid to speak. Angelou somehow felt that by revealing to her uncles what had happened to her caused another tragedy. The story infers that the uncles killed the perpetrator. Angelou in turn decided to stay caged up within herself. Similarly, although African Americans have been emancipated, some have refused to accept their liberation and make life work for them.

Progress has been made in the Black church and communities over the last century but is followed by a backlash. Many African Americans have decided to speak up and speak out against social and economic injustice. However, some have become bitter and even violent. As we continue to witness young Black men and women gunned down by law enforcement, hiding behind a statement of fear for their lives, is it really fear, or a form of keeping the Jim Crow laws alive? The tremendous gains made by formerly enslaved Blacks were undercut by the establishment of Jim Crow. The revolutionary legal victories won by the brave women and men of the twentieth-century Civil Rights Movement were undermined by the harsh, racial politics of Nixon and Reagan (especially their "War on Drugs"). The first Black president of the United States was succeeded by a man who promotes racism and division versus equality and unity. Racism and xenophobia of immense proportions are being flaunted without care, with individuals emboldened by tacit support from the highest levels of US society.

According to Knabb and Pelletier (2014), Religion and spirituality can be powerful supports and provide important coping resources for the Black community. Faith communities seem to offer many advantages for those living in poverty. It appears that religious communities are a frontier in psychological service. Basic helpful interventions such as psychoeducation, coping skills, and increased interpersonal connection are ideal for implementation in a religious community setting (Rogers, and Stanford 2015). Church-sponsored resources have been shown to be effective at delivering these types of interventions and have the added benefits of minimal cost and maximum accessibility (Rogers and Stanford 2015). We are continuously dealing with obstacles and conflicts throughout our life—regardless if it is within church, career work groups, or in our personal life. Change in the Black church and community will transpire when the Spiritual leaders take the initiative to lead. In concluding this book, I share a paradigm shift of a community living in poverty.

The Dudley Street Neighborhood Initiative

Social organization theory suggests that place matters (Rogers, 2013). A person's residential location contributes a large part of illegal participation. (Rogers, 2013). In relating to Dudley Street Community neighborhood, residents fought against festering criminal activities on the streets (Holding ground part 2, 2010).

One example of steps the community initiated to increase efficacy was to alleviate vacant lots where drug activities were prevalent (Holding ground part 2, 2010). The residents decided to go to their city officials and solicited support to clean up the vacant lot (Holding ground part 2, 2010). The vacant lots were filled with garbage and other types of debris. Still, another example the residents initiated were to rebuild their communities to include, shopping centers and decent and affordable homes (Holding ground part 2, 2010). By reconstructing the neighborhood, the residents believed that this would decrease criminal activities and attract working-class citizens (Holding ground part 2, 2010).

The residents also motivated the young individuals to get involved in the initiative. The young individuals played a vital role in cleaning up their community, while developing self-worth among themselves. The residents were concerned that the buildup of trash and crime would have a negative physiological effect on their children. The residents were also concerned that the children would be affected by the criminal activities that were prevalent in the drug-infested neighborhood (Holding ground part 2, 2010).

Community organization theory applies to the Dudley Street Neighborhood Initiative, in that the residents demanded social justice and social change (Rogers, 2013). The residents used social action strategies by involving city and state officials in the Initiative (Holding ground part 2, 2010). The residents solicited nonprofit agencies support as well. Residents of Dudley Street developed self-help groups to boost morale among their community participants (Holding ground part 2, 2010).

A second theory that applies to the Dudley Street Neighborhood Initiative is racism, discrimination, and social and economic oppression (Rogers, 2013). The residents of Dudley Street were compiled of diverse races. The residents experienced racism on the micro, macro, and mezzo levels, because of lack of wealth and power. The residents experienced discrimination because of their race and ethnicity.

The evident intervention utilized in the Dudley Street Initiative is that the initial movement did not include any of the Dudley Street residents. The initial board members were compiled of mostly Caucasian males, who did not live in the neighborhood (Holding ground part 2, 2010). One board member admitted that he judged Chez, who was one of the outspoken residents, as an agitator (Holding ground part 2, 2010). The effective interventions utilized in the Initiative were the residents coming together, regardless of language barriers, and were a positive show of community organization.

The Dudley Street Neighborhood Initiative employed resources from the residents. The residents worked together to clean their neighborhood. The residents sought support from the city of Boston to initiate a greater cleanup effort. The nonprofit officials solicited grants from government entities. Eventually, The Dudley Street Initiative received 34 million dollars from public funding (Holding ground part 2, 2010). Social policies such as, Boston Promise Initiative were initiated to ensure further progress for the Dudley Community. (Sklar, 1996). The Dudley Street Neighborhood Initiative was also assisted by Citizen Participation in Boston's Development Policy: The Political Economy of Participation (Urban Affairs, 1995).

My community and other communities require collaboration from Black leaders and systems that consist of interdependent parts. When combined to make an organized whole of eliminating poverty, the cycle of poverty in the Black church and community can be addressed. This transpired in the Dudley Street Neighborhood, and it could happen in your neighborhood as well.

References

Adams, M., Blumenfeld, W. J., Castaneda, C., Hackman, H. W., Peters, M. L., & Zuniga, X. (Eds.). (2013). Readings for diversity and social justice. (3rd ed.). New York, NY: Routledge Press.

Akella, D., & Jordan, M. (2015). Impact of Social and Cultural Factors on Teen Pregnancy. Journal of Health Disparities Research & Practice, 8(1), 41-61.

Benjamin, E., Constantine, E., Richardson, T., Wilson, J. (1998). An overview of Black racial identity theories: Limitations and considerations for future theoretical conceptualizations. Applied and Preventive Psychology,

Brien, M. J., Loya, G. E., & Pepper, J. V. (2002). Teenage childbearing and cognitive development. Journal of Population Economics, 15(3), 391.

Business & Economics Research – June 2013 Volume 11, Number 6
http://www.ebony.com/news-views/the-relentless-poverty-of-albany-georgia-981#ixzz4NX4osV9b
http://freeclinicdirectory.org/georgia_care/dougherty_ga_county.html.
http://www.walb.com/story/24474941/.

Cone, James H. A Black Theology of Liberation. Maryknoll, NY: Orbis, 2010.

———. Black Theology and Black Power. Maryknoll, NY: Orbis, 1997.

———. God of the Oppressed. Maryknoll, NY: Orbis, 1997.

———. The Cross and the Lynching Tree. Maryknoll, NY: Orbis, 2011.

———. "Theology's Great Sin: Silence in the Face of White Supremacy." Black Theology: An International Journal 2.2 (2004): 139–152.

———. The Spirituals and the Blues: An Interpretation. Maryknoll, NY: Orbis, 1991.

Cross, William E. (1995). "The Black Identity Model." Black World 20 (9)13–27. Refere Development Graduate Programs website: http://www.planning.org/policy/guides/adopted/homelessness.htm

De Genna, N., Larkby, C., & Cornelius, M. (2011). Pubertal Timing and Early Sexual Intercourse in the Offspring of Teenage Mothers. Journal of Youth & Adolescence, 40(10), 1315-1328 14p. doi:10.1007/s10964-010-9609-3

Duba, J. D. (2005). Integrative and Biopsychosocial Therapy: An Interview with Len Sperry, M.D., Ph.D. The Family Journal, 13(1), 101-106. doi:10.1177/1066480704270131

D.M. Griffith, M. Mason, M. Yonas, E. Eng, V. Jeffries, S. Plihcik, B. Parks **Dismantling institutional racism: theory and action** Am. J. Community Psychol., 39 (2007), pp. 381-392, 10.1007/s10464-007-9117-0 (Holding ground part 2, 2010) Dudley Street Neighborhood Initiative/ Winthrop Estates. Planning, 63(4), 6.

Hansan, J.E. (2013). Josephine Shaw Lowell (1843-1905) — Social reformer, founder of the New York City Charity Organization Society and advocate of the doctrine that charity should not merely relieve suffering but that it should also rehabilitate the recipient. Social Welfare History Project. Retrieved [date accessed] from http://socialwelfare.library.vcu.edu/organizations/state-institutions/lowell-josephine-shaw-3/

Ichiro, S., & Tomio, K. (2015). A Theory for Complex System's Social Change: An Application of a Generally 'Critically' Model. Interdisciplinary Description of Complex Systems, 13(3),34353. doi:10.7906/indecs.13.3.1

Knabb, J. J., & Pelletier, J. (2014). "A Cord of Three Strands is Not Easily Broken"

Kondrat, M. (2002). Actor-centered social work: re-visioning 'person-in-environment' through a critical theory lens. Social Work, 47(4), 435-448 14p. doi: sw/47.4.435

Ichiro, S., & Tomio, K. (2015). A Theory for Complex System's Social Change: An Application of a Generally 'Critically' Model. Interdisciplinary Description of Complex Systems, 13(3), 342-353. doi:10.7906/indecs.13.3.1

Lee, Y. (2013). Adolescent Motherhood and Capital: Interaction Effects of Race/Ethnicity on Harsh Parenting.

Rogers, A. (2013). Human Behavior in the Social Environment. Hoboken: Routledge.

Rogers, E. B., & Stanford, M. S. (2015). A church-based peer-led group intervention for mental illness. Mental Health, Religion & Culture, 18(6), 470-481 12p. doi:10.1080/13674676.2015.1077560 19(3), 24-27 4p.

Sklar, H. (1996). Building an urban village: The Dudley Street Neighborhood Initiative. Environmental Action, 28(1/2), 33.

Sue, D. W. (2006). Multicultural social work practice. Hoboken, NJ : Wiley, c2006.

Suls, J., Krantz, D. S., & Williams, G. C. (2013). Three strategies for bridging distinct levels of analysis and embracing the biopsychosocial model. Health Psychology, 32(5), 597-601. doi:10.1037/a0031197

Urban Affairs Review, (1995). 30:514-537

Vandiver, B. J., Cross, W. E. Jr., Fhagen-Smith, P. E., Worrell, F. C., Swim, J., & Caldwell, L. (2001). The Cross Racial Identity Scale. Unpublished scale

Zastrow, C. H., & Kirst-Ashman, K. K. (2016). Understanding human behavior and the social environment (10th ed.). Boston, MA: Cengage Learning.